DAILY
BOUQUET

David Watts

Nicholas David
Publications San Francisco,
London

Cover art...............................Gabriel Baranow-Watts
Cover design.......................................Kevin Diamond
Book Design...Lauren Gonzalez

FIRST EDITION

You can observe a lot by watching.
Yogi Berra

DAILY BOUQUET

not the flowers
but that you brought them

the closure of arms around
an embrace
is also an opening

we are tumbling through the
universe
on a curve ball

the kiss is a door that wants to open

teenage lasts from thirteen to fifty

paddle upstream first

sacred ground is anywhere you were
young
and barefoot

old age takes a lot of years and
comes on early

shrink wrap is impossible to open

aliens are probably nicer than we are

the natural state of a garden hose is
tangled

less trouble to be kind
than to undo a cruelty

by starting again you can change
the ending

no such thing as a kept secret

to understand your parents
you have to raise children

if you're missing happiness go back
to where you left it

from the day they were born
your children were members of a
different culture

avoid sex in old age
and you'll know what it's like to be
dead

an apology has no but

if you don't like the present
wait a second and it will be the past

everybody has moral restrictions,
except the Supreme Court

before you blame yourself check
for assholes in the room

be an optimist; the other path is not well-lit

part of love is doing the hard things together

the brain informs but the heart decides

we are always working on a version
of ourselves

a little distance makes you closer

the faces at a reunion have been
toasted a little
in the oven of time

failures come like junk mail
laughter like rain

much deserves forgetting

time is just a place with a strange address

you can't blame the answer
if you asked the question

it takes considerable attachment
to want to clean a room

what the future holds
is how the past
changed its mind

love turns the clock back

chili pepper is a game of chance

not every crackle on the roof is a raindrop
not every eye contact is an invitation

the rigid idea is easily fooled

good reasons don't always justify
the action

the winter cherry still remembers
how to fruit

beauty always contains a little
sorrow

forgiveness is an act of grace, no one must earn it.

insomnia is a disruption with its tail
wagging

each tear is a message in a bottle

if we are not acquainted with illness
we will be afraid of it

silence asks the right questions

simultaneous thoughts are no accident
among lovers and friends

start with trust, then modify

lectures are off-putting, stories engage

crooked politicians are popular
because they validate our dark side

words are little hypodermics of meaning

love is how far your circles overlap;
some things you share,
some things you don't

a mask allows you to be dangerous

you will never convince some people
of the truth;
this is also true of relatives

if you can love don't save it

less bullshitting would help

stupidity has no doubts

the brain is a muscle that likes exercise

be sure what you have to say is
better than silence

careful what you predict

a period points in all directions

the universe has questions too

sometimes the answer does the asking

the ideas you want
are the ones that crack you open

passion defeats procrastination

words vaguely resemble what happened

some politicians believe in divine
corruption

some friendships last forever
some wash away with soap

our glances leave weight on the skin

each year is smaller

a smile doesn't have to understand
anything

dance speaks words that words
cannot say

action has the appearance of competence

intelligence is larger when it lies low

success is all hard work and mostly
luck

progress tanks when congress
comes to town

ask any child, they're smarter

children have a second stomach for
dessert

love is able to say I let you go

every small leaving is tender

the universe has an imagination too

rumors inflate the negative

the wind is someone we once knew

the best poets ask the best questions

if you can't get rid of anxiety
make a place for it at the table

memoir and fiction are both true

love is like snowflakes, each is
different

love is not love that cannot be
deepened by sorrow

no guardrails in a divorce court

dreams are travels of the spirit

don't ask a question if your
bladder's full

nothing like winning an election
to destroy your sense of morality

optimists make the best cynics

like poison oak
hatred does its damage
before you know what it is

when bodies touch music is not far
behind

few demons have the strength
to finish the job

the holy bow to those less fortunate

in the dark of winter
remember spring
will weave her carpet of light

each dinner date is a floor plan
for a mansion

someone inside us is always kissing
somebody

even the broken reed can sing

. . . With Inspiration From:

Rumi, Yogi Berra, Hafez, Calvin and Hobbs,

and the vast unconscious mind.

harvey ellis

"I have loved getting these .... a mind hug in the mornings."

"Agree or not, David Watts composes delicious mental chewing gum."

"Each of these pearls of wisdom is a complete movie."